Quaker Faith & Practice around the world

"You will say, Christ said this and the apostles say this, but what can you say? Are you a child of the Light and have walked in the Light; and what you speak, is it inwardly from God?"

George Fox, speaking in the Ulverston steeplehouse, 1652

A study guide for Friends

ISBN 0-901856-09-6

978-0-901856-09-8

Published by the *World Gathering of Young Friends Charitable Committee*, May 2005

Copyleft 2005 World Gathering of Young Friends Charitable Committee — you are free to copy any part of this book for non-profit purposes so long as you include this copyleft notice and attribute sources in any extract quoted. Extracts from Quaker Books of Discipline reproduced under the the Fair Use principle of Article 10 of the Berne Convention.

All enquiries to simon gray, simon@star-one.org.uk

ISBN 0-901856-09-6 (978-0-901856-09-8)

Prepared, designed, and typeset by *simon gray*

With thanks to *Aidan McCartney, Anna Dunford, Anneke Spreij, Bainito Wamalwa, Betsy Blake, Hanna Nohe, Helen Close, Jaime Tobingo, John Fitzgerald, & Marie-Helene Drouin*

Cover photograph: Pont Mileniwm / Millennium Bridge, Machynclleth, Wales

Set in 10pt Tahoma & Trebuchet MS; a large print version is available at www.wgyf.org/faithandpractice.pdf or by post

Printed by Westpoint Printing, Digbeth, Birmingham, UK

Contents

Quaker Faith and Practice
around the world

In this book we shall take a look at what Friends around the world think, do, and believe specifically by way of the writings of Quakers as compiled in the various *Books of Discipline*, or *Faith and Practices* as used in many of the different yearly meetings around the world.

The **Queries for discussion** at the end of each section are intended to be used as a starting point – do not feel restricted to using only those ones; indeed, it is hoped that many more queries will arise from study of the material. Use them, and this book itself, both for personal reflection and study and also for wider discussion amongst small groups. When studying in groups you may find it helpful to read the extracts aloud in the same manner as a Bible study session in order to help the group focus on the text itself.

Don't stop at the extracts quoted here – if your yearly meeting's book of discipline is not represented in any given section (or overall), seek out some extracts from it too which speak to the topics covered. Make an effort to find other extracts from other *Faith and Practices* which are also relevant. Think of other broader subjects on which Friends traditionally have had something specific to say, and seek out a selection of extracts which talk about those. The *Online Faith & Practice* website at **http://worship.quaker.org/qfp** is a particularly valuable resource for this.

It is hoped by studying material from *Faith and Practice* around the Quaker world the reader will not only gain a greater insight into how Friends live their witness in traditions other than their own, but also gain a deeper understanding and interest in the contents of their own book of discipline.

In this study there is no doctrinal or theological 'bias' to be inferred – this study does not aim to dictate what is true. That is for you and your worshipping community to discern. Be honest with yourself and with the wider group.

1: What is Quaker Faith and Practice?

Some yearly meetings place greater importance on their *Book of Discipline* than others, and indeed many yearly meetings don't have such a book at all - so since some people may not even be well acquainted with their own yearly meeting's book let alone others', it is a good idea for us to first be clear what it actually is.

Most yearly meetings who have such a book tend to have it split into two parts – sometimes physically split, but usually bound together in the same volume. The first part is the yearly meeting's formal constitutional document – its 'book of rules' which governs such procedural matters as marriages and funerals, membership procedures, the appointment of elders, pastors, overseers, and clerks etc. Often it outlines the responsibilities of various roles within a meeting, and informs how the various committees and groups which make up the wider organisation relate to each other and what they do. This part is usually called something like *Church Government*, or the *Handbook of Practice and Procedure*.

The other part is effectively 'our story'. It is a collection of inspirational writings of various individual Friends, and groups of Friends, through to minutes of meetings, to statements which all of us at our annual main meeting for church affairs and beyond have made on various aspects of what it means to be a Quaker today. Some of the writings included are modern, and some of them date from the earliest years of Quakerism. Topics covered include social justice issues, education, faith and action, bereavement, relationships and sexuality, Friends and the State, peace, Meeting for Worship, creativity, suffering, simplicity, and just about anything else you can think of and how it relates to our spirituality.

Many yearly meetings also have in their books a section called something like *Advices and Queries, Questions and Counsel,* or *Queries for Serious Consideration* – this is a smaller part which can often be said to be the distillation of the whole of the wider volume and the collective wisdom of the yearly meeting into one short section (which is often published as a separate pamphlet); if you want to know where any given yearly meeting is 'at', this is usually a good place to start. The queries are the way each

Quaker community calls its members to account – sometimes overtly, sometimes subtly; and the advices are just that – good advice on life and conduct for the struggling and not-so-struggling Friend.

Not all yearly meetings call their book of discipline *Quaker Faith and Practice* – in Australia the book is called *this we can say – Australian Quaker Life, Faith, and Thought*, and in Ireland it is called *Christian Experience*. Not all yearly meetings have their own book, and will use the book of another yearly meeting with which they are in spiritual or organisational sympathy. Wherever Friends are as a whole on the Christocentric / Universalist spectrum, the book of discipline is not used a replacement for the *Bible* and is not considered to be divinely inspired; more it is thought of as the statement of what makes us uniquely Friends together in our spiritual paths.

Queries for discussion

Are you aware of the importance or otherwise the book of discipline plays generally in the life of your own yearly meeting?

Does it play more, less, or a roughly equal part in your own personal spiritual journey?

Do you have your 'favourite quotes' from it?

Do you try to be aware of the whole of your yearly meeting's book of discipline?

Are there any parts of it which you find uncomfortable, less interesting, or inapplicable to your own situation and interests?

2: The way we talk to one another

Even in our own meetings at home we don't always agree with what others say. Here are a few passages from around the world which try to help us handle disagreement and debate in a manner befitting our testimonies.

1: "Do you refrain from verbal and psychological violence? And when people attack you with angry words, do you listen for the underlying hurt?

Take thought for the words you use, and the tones of voice in which you utter them. Corruption and destructiveness can grow from very small seeds; and so can courage and loving kindness". *Aotearoa New Zealand Yearly Meeting, Questions and Counsel, D9.*

2: "We must resist the temptation to be possessively attached to our own ideas. Christ will teach us what we need to know to perform his service, but not to satisfy our curiosity or to encourage us in building theories. We are advised to bear in mind that what we think we know is often influenced by hearsay, faulty memory, or the climate of opinion among our immediate associates. Opinions should be held modestly if at all, and they should not become the occasion of arguments. In speaking what we feel God has led us to assert, we should speak forthrightly, but avoid laying stress on our personal claim to revelation, allowing the power of Truth to accompany its own message". *Friends of Truth / Glenside Friends Meeting, Christian Conduct, Opinions.*

3: "Do you respect that of God in everyone though it may be expressed in unfamiliar ways or be difficult to discern? Each of us has a particular experience of God and each must find the way to be true to it. When words are strange or disturbing to you, try to sense where they come from and what has nourished the lives of others. Listen patiently and seek the truth which other people's opinions may contain for you. Avoid hurtful criticism and provocative language. Do not allow the strength of your convictions to betray you into making statements or allegations that are unfair or untrue. Think it possible that you may be mistaken". *Britain Yearly Meeting, Advices and Queries, 17*

4: "As followers of Christ do you love and respect each other? Do patience and consideration govern your interactions; and when differences arise, do you resolve them promptly in a spirit of forgiveness and understanding? Are you careful with the reputation of others?" *Northwest Yearly Meeting, The Queries, Query 6.*

5: "Do you cherish an understanding and forgiving spirit? Do you avoid unkind gossip and the spreading of rumour? Do you avoid damaging the reputation of others? Do you cultivate an appreciation of each individual's worth?" *Ireland Yearly Meeting, Queries for Serious Consideration, 6*

6: "All are especially cautioned against any harshness of tone or manner when administering counsel or reproof, either privately or in meetings. Friends should speak truth with love, remembering that if they would do God's work, they must abide in God's love. Even a seeming harshness may check the beginnings of true repentance, and a lack of sympathy may cause harm where only good was intended". *New York Yearly Meeting, Advices, 15*

Queries for discussion

Do you enjoy a good debate or discussion, whether based on faith, politics, social issues, or other concerns?

A free flowing discussion can be interesting and robust and still take place according to the Friends' principles expressed above - do you allow yourself to express your own views in a forthright manner which still shows love and respect for your fellows?

Can you think of an occasion when you fell short of the principles above?

Are you aware of how others might have felt then?

When do you feel you have shown your values in action during debate? What were the topics of those discussions?

3: Personal devotion and prayer

In the Quaker life it is as important to spend time in quiet reflection upon God as it is to take part in public worship. Sometimes, to pray is to talk to God, to ask God to intercede in the affairs of humanity; on other occasions prayer is about listening to God, and about submitting to God's will.

1: "A walk with God cannot be maintained without prayer. Let none allow the rush of engagements or the hurry of business to crowd out their opportunities for private retirement and waiting upon God. Prayer is not limited to time or place or the utterance of words. Amidst the pressure of daily life the breathing of the soul toward God will receive a gracious answer from Him; and they who thus live in the spirit of prayer will also find it to their joy an atmosphere of praise. [...]

The duty and privilege of prayer are clearly set forth in the Holy Scriptures. Prayer is the aspiration of the heart unto God: it is the first and natural impulse of the awakened soul; and it becomes the habitual exercise of those whose lives are guided by the fear and love of God". *Ireland Yearly Meeting, Christian Experience, Chapter 6: Private Retirement and Prayer*

2: "We believe in God the Holy Spirit, who enables us to have direct union, communication, and communion with God, and who brings true inward witness and spiritual renewal without prompting of symbols or ceremonial rites (*Acts 1:15*)" *East Africa Yearly Meeting North, Faith and Practice, The Statement of Faith*

3: "A sense of need is a sufficient call to prayer. Hence the burdened sinner may come boldly to the throne of grace and find a welcoming Father from whom he can obtain forgiveness. Similarly the burdened Christian can find in prayer the assurance of God's love and relief from his burden as he casts all his care on the Lord (*I Peter 5:7*)

Prayer is the life breath of Christian living and gives the Christian unbroken access to his heavenly Father. It is thus essential to the maintenance and development of the Christian life. We believe that it should be the daily exercise of the individual Christians within our fellowship that our families should set apart time for collective prayer, Bible reading and praise and that in our public services of worship we should give importance to prayer and praise". *Philippines Evangelical Friends Church, Statement of Faith and Christian Practice*

4: "In a recent radio broadcast an Islamic theologian said that in the view of Islam 'the practice of medicine is an act of worship, a manifestation of the principle of unity (of body, mind and spirit)'. My mind turned to a moment in my life not long past.

I was sitting at the bedside of our granddaughter, who had hovered for 48 hours between life and death with meningitis and was now lying apparently unseeing, unhearing, shallowly breathing. I sang to her one of her favourite nursery songs and, as always, I got a particular word wrong. She opened her eyes, corrected me (as always), gave me a beautiful smile and relapsed to her former state.

Hilary, at two and a half years of age, was a child of exhilarating vitality, full of dance and song, living life as it were on tiptoe and loving everyone. The threat of death was succeeded by statistical probabilities: damage to brain, sight, hearing and/or mobility. Ultimately she left hospital with just a limp, which slowly disappeared, restoring her former exuberance to the full.

I do not understand the nature of spiritual healing. What words can convey a mystery? What heart can deny it, once experienced? I had no evidence that Hilary would not have recovered, or not so well, in the absence of prayer. I do not picture a God who is deciding who shall live, who shall die and when, and who is influenced in this task by our entreaties. But the experience with Hilary has strengthened my belief that the healing acts of Jesus were not a demonstration of special status, but an illustration of the working of the Spirit through ordinary people. There is a strength, an empowerment, to be channelled through prayer". *Australia Yearly Meeting, this we can say, 3.13*

5: "My own belief is that outward circumstances are not often (I will not say **never**) directly altered as a result of prayer. That is to say, God is not always interfering with the working of the natural order. But indirectly by the working of mind upon mind great changes may be wrought. We live and move and have our being in God; we are bound up in the bundle of life in Him, and it is reasonable to believe that prayer may often find its answer, even in outward things, by the reaction of mind upon mind. Prayer is not given us to make life easy for us, or to coddle us, but to make us strong ... to make us masters of circumstances and not its slaves. We pray, not to change God's will, but to bring our wills into correspondence with His". *Britain Yearly Meeting, Quaker Faith and Practice, 2.24*

6: "'I think a quiet spirit before the Lord and not always looking out for "concerns," but knowing how to be still, is a very great point in the religious life'. (*Elizabeth Fry, Memoirs of Elizabeth Fry, 1847*)

Nurturing the life of the Spirit requires frequent communication with the Divine Spirit. It is not sufficient to rely solely on an hour (or less) on First Day mornings, or on brief moments of silence before meals or committee meetings. We should make room in each day to know that of God within ourselves. God's help and healing can be sought in many ways, including vocal or silent prayer, meditation, visualization, silent listening, and confident affirmation. Friends seek harmony with the Divine Will, individually or in groups, sometimes laying our concerns before God, sometimes asking for guidance, sometimes giving thanks for the beauty and blessing in our lives". *Baltimore Yearly Meeting, Faith and Practice, Advices: The Life of the Spirit - 5. Prayer and Meditation*

Queries for discussion

Do you set aside time in your life for personal devotion?

What does prayer mean to you in your everyday life?

What form do your prayers take?

How does prayer help you with difficult issues?

How do you think God responds to your prayers?

Can you think of an example when God has answered?

What do you do during your times of personal devotion?

How has personal devotion affected your relationship with and understanding of God?

4: Quaker business meetings

As well as meeting to worship together, part of the responsibility of being a member of a Quaker community is to take part in the making of decisions - ranging from our small committees through to our local and yearly meetings, and sometimes even as part of the global family of Friends.

1: "Friends' business meetings are meetings for worship with a concern for business. When there seems to be disagreement, a free expression of all opinions should be encouraged. Those who speak in meetings for business are advised not to be unduly persistent in advocacy or opposition, but, after having fully expressed their views, to recognize the generally expressed sense of the meeting. A deep and seeking silence can help to reconcile seemingly opposing points of view. Meetings should be conducted in the spirit of wisdom, forbearance, and love". *New York Yearly Meeting, Advices, 16*

2: "Friends wishing to speak indicate this by standing or raising a hand. They speak only when called on to do so by the Clerk, and stand if possible. Speakers try to be concise and to the point confining themselves to the issue before the Meeting. Persons should try to speak only once upon one topic considering carefully what they say and not repeating points already made. Queries and points of clarification should be addressed through the Clerk.

Friends listen to what is being said and allow a 'cushion of silence' before there is a further contribution.

A Friends Meeting is not a debating forum or a town meeting where everyone has the right to speak... no one has the right to speak in Meeting - rather Friends have the privilege and the duty to lay before the Meeting what ever relevant insight they may possess. And whatever has been laid before the Meeting needs to be considered carefully and belongs to the Meeting not the individual". *Central and Southern Africa Yearly Meeting, Handbook of Practice and Procedure, Friends' Meeting for Business*

3: "In making decisions at business meeting we seek to reach unity about the issue at hand, knowing that the Spirit of Christ by which alone we can rightly be led, is one and is not

in contradiction to itself. When unity cannot be reached it is ordinarily necessary to delay action until it can. Sometimes a member may have less clarity than others about a proposed decision but feel that he or she should not oppose it; in such case the church may decide that it has sufficient unity to proceed. Members must be wary, however, of acquiescing to proposals out of a dislike of disagreeing with others; it may be any member's responsibility to voice hesitation about the rightness of an impending decision.

Members should be slow to speak and avoid interrupting one another, and at times leave pauses between speakers so that the full import of what has been said may be absorbed. This happens spontaneously when all are in the right spirit". *Friends of Truth / Glenside Friends Meeting, Meeting for Business*

4: "Do we enter into Meeting for Worship for Business in a spirit of worship and inward peace?

Do we feel gathered in the presence of God in meeting for business and trust our corporate guidance?

Do we listen and share in a spirit of forbearance and charity toward others?

Are we sensitive in pressing our views?

Are we mindful of seeking the corporate sense of the meeting?

Are we able to feel in unity with the spirit of the meeting even when our own opinions and ideas differ from the opinions and ideas of others?

Are we patient when the process of discernment by the meeting seems slow or stalled?

Are we able to open ourselves in prayer to the promptings of the Spirit and to follow a new path in search of unity?

Do we experience a sense of inner peace when the meeting has concluded its consideration of a matter and has made a decision?" *Australia Yearly Meeting, this we can say, 2.43*

5: "Both in meetings for worship and in meetings for business we search for the lead of the Spirit of Truth and Life, in an atmosphere of love and unity. In these meetings we understand that it is possible to reach decisions in unity.

When a serious case of disagreement occurs and tempers are short, the clerk or any other Friend can ask the group to have some time of silent or waiting worship in order to look for God's lead to inspire this necessary unity.

The method requires patience, love and comprehension from all present, taking into account the rights of the minority - although in reality there is no minority or majority, but a group which endeavours to reach unity by looking for God's Will". *Cuba Yearly Meeting, Faith and Practice*

6: "Decisions do not need to be unanimous, but they do need substantial unity. Members who disagree with an action may 'stand aside', that is, agree to let the others proceed without their agreeing with the action taken. Those who stand aside are also agreeing not to become divisive and not to oppose the implementation of the decision. On rare occasions, when the issue is grave and a decision must be made, those who disagree may ask to have their names registered in the minutes as opposing the action.

The Friends method of doing business is sometimes slow, but it does build unity. At its best, it is beautiful to watch the Holy Spirit bring a group to unity. That's why the spirit of authentic worship, and seeking the mind of Christ Jesus who is always present, is so vital". *Evangelical Friends Church Southwest, Faith and Practice, Friends way of doing business*

Queries for discussion

Do you regularly go to business meetings in your Quaker community? If not, why not?

Are there any recurring business items which you find less interesting?

Do you ever stop concentrating in a business session?

Have you ever had to present an item to a business meeting?

Have you ever felt your ministry in a business session was not properly heard?

How does the practice of 'standing aside from the minute' as held in some yearly meetings sit with you?

Have there ever been any occasions you felt particularly pleased because your contribution seemed to set the sense of the meeting?

5: Spiritual gifts

Friends have always had a particular concern for the recognition and cherishing of spiritual gifts. They place special emphasis on the responsibility of the meeting's members to ensure the ongoing work and nurture of our communities.

1: "Be earnestly concerned to use the spiritual gifts entrusted to you faithfully and to the honor of God.

In the exercise of the ministry, wait for the renewed putting forth of the Holy Spirit; be careful not to exceed the measure of your gifts, but proceed and conclude in the spirit and authority of the Gospel.

In your spoken ministry, be concerned to present the life and teaching of Christ Jesus, the Lord, reverently seeking wisdom from God, that you may be enabled rightly to interpret the Word of Truth. Let nothing be done or offered with a view to popularity, but all in humility and love.

Bearing in mind that the treasure is in earthen vessels, beware of laying stress on your ministry, the baptizing power of the Spirit of Truth accompanying the Word being the true evidence.

Be tender at all times of each other's reputation, and watchful lest you hurt each other's service as servants of the same Lord, with diversities of gifts, but the same spirit. Maintain a lively exercise harmoniously to labor for the spreading and advancement of the truth.

Let ministers endeavor to express themselves audibly and distinctly, and guard against tones and gestures inconsistent with Christian gravity and simplicity. Let them beware of using unnecessary preambles and of making unneeded additions toward the conclusion of a meeting.

When traveling in the service of Christ, be careful to move under His guidance. Let your visits be neither short and hurried, nor long and burdensome, nor unnecessarily expensive. Give no offense in anything, that the ministry be not blamed.

Prayer and thanksgiving are an important part of worship. May they be offered in spirit and in truth, with a right understanding, seasoned with grace. When engaged therein, avoid many words and repetitions, and be cautious of too often repeating the High and Holy Name of God. Neither let prayer be in a formal and customary way, nor without a reverent sense of Divine guidance.

Finally, dear Friends, take heed to yourselves and to all the flock amongst whom you have been called to labor. Be faithful, be patient, be in earnest to fulfill your appointed service, that when the Chief Shepherd shall appear, you may receive the crown of glory that fadeth not away". *North Carolina Yearly Meeting (Conservative), Faith and Practice, Advices to meeting of ministry and oversight*

2: "Friends believe in the gifts of the Spirit as taught by Paul in *1 Corinthians 12* and *Ephesians 4*. We believe that the gifts listed by Paul and in evidence elsewhere in the New Testament record are distributed according to God's plan among all Christians – old and young, male and female, among those who are illiterate and those of advanced education or physical disability. Spiritual gifts are abilities or capacities which are intended by God to help build up the church – to teach, lead, inspire, pastor, heal, assist, administer, comfort, correct, pray for others. Our spiritual leaders should be chosen by our churches based on evidence that they have the spiritual gifts appropriate for their office.

Spiritual gifts, when used under the guidance and leadership of the Holy Spirit, are to be respected by others." *Friends United Meeting in East Africa, Christian Faith and Practice in the Friends Church, Spiritual Gifts.*

3: "Every Friend is called to be a servant of God. Each of us has God-given gifts or talents, which we are obliged to develop and use to the glory of God. Each of us is encouraged to seek the ways in which we are called to minister to others. 'Speak, for thy servant hears', is our prayer (*I Samuel 3:10*).

We are obliged also to recognize and nurture the gifts of other Friends. The spiritual quality of our meetings for worship deepens when those who are led to speak out of the silence receive encouragement and help. The fabric of the Meeting community and the larger community is strengthened when Friends who serve the community receive loving support from other Friends.

Monthly Meetings may wish to recognize in some way the special gifts of certain Friends, in the ministry of the word, in Bible interpretation, First Day School teaching, peace witness, prison visiting, counseling or the like. One way is to acknowledge the gift in the minutes of the Meeting. Such formal recognition expresses approval of the Friend's contribution and may affirm his or her suitability to interpret the Society of Friends to the larger community.

Some Meetings may choose to continue the historical practice of recording ministers. Meetings wishing to acknowledge gifts in ministry by recording may consult the Yearly Meeting Committee on Nurture and Recognition of Ministry". *Baltimore Yearly Meeting, Advices, The Life of the Spirit – 4:Use and Nurture of Gifts*

4: "Friends believe that spiritual gifts are bestowed by the Holy Spirit for the propagation of the Gospel, for the perfection of believers, and for the edifying of the church in faith and power. In seeking the baptism with the Holy Spirit, Friends have sought not so much to receive a particular gift as to be controlled by the Giver of the gifts. Even so, it is recognized that the Spirit gives different gifts to different members of the body of Christ (*Romans 12*). The exercise of these gifts brings Christ's truth to personal consciousness in varied ways appropriate to need. Accordingly, sharp distinctions between different types of ministry should not be attempted. Persons may have multiple gifts, exercised at different times, both through ordinary abilities sanctified to divine use and through extraordinary sensitivities and actions.

Friends believe that gifts are for God's glory and that enduement of power must be subordinate to purity. Friends also believe that the baptism with the Holy Spirit brings heart cleansing and conformity to the image of Christ (*Acts 15:8*). In *Hebrews 12: 14* we are asked to "make every effort to live in peace with all men and be holy: without holiness no one shall see the Lord." For evidence of the presence of the Holy Spirit Friends are exhorted to look to inner transformation. This transformation empowers the believer to live in victory over wilful sin and produces a

condition of love, shown outwardly by the fruit of the Spirit and Christian graces". *Northwest Yearly Meeting, Faith and Practice, Fundamental Truths*

5: "In order to facilitate and expand pastoral and other activities within and outside the meeting, it is the practice of some meetings to employ the services of people who can devote time to this work. Meetings may designate such people as pastors, meeting secretaries, or counselors.

Pastors, who are usually recorded ministers, are expected to serve the meeting in the field of public ministry, although they should always have due regard for other ministers in the meeting and for visiting Friends who have service to render. Due consideration should also be given to the value of silent worship and freedom of expression, vital to group worship. Pastors and meeting secretaries are co-workers with the members of the meeting, developing and encouraging initiative and the assumption of responsibility by the members, who are also called to minister according to their gifts". *New York Yearly Meeting, Faith and Practice, Functions of Ministry and Counsel*

6: "The priesthood is for all believers, according to the gifts of the Holy Spirit (*Eph. 4:11-16*) but pastoral leadership has an important role and function in our churches. Pastors who are trained and qualified are to give spiritual and pastoral leadership to all our churches. Churches and yearly meetings must care financially and otherwise for their pastors". *East Africa Yearly Meeting North, Faith and Practice, The Statement of Faith*

7: "'Now there are a variety of gifts, but the same Spirit; and there are a variety of services, but the same Lord; and there are varieties of activities, but it is the same God who activates all of them in everyone. To each is given the manifestation of the Spirit for the common good'. (*I Cor 12:4-7*)

It is a responsibility of a Christian community to enable its members to discover what their gifts are and to develop and exercise them to the glory of God". *Britain Yearly Meeting, Quaker Faith and Practice, 3.22*

Queries for discussion

How good are you at recognising your own spiritual gifts?

Do you acknowledge the spiritual gifts of others?

What kinds of things do you consider to be spiritual gifts, and where do you think they are displayed?

Are there other gifts which you would not consider to be spiritual gifts? Why?

What do you think are the barriers to the full development and display of anybody's spiritual gifts?

Do you feel your Friends' community takes its full responsibility in supporting and caring for those amongst you who display and act on their gifts?

What areas for improvement can you see in this - and what part can you play to bring that about?

6: Peace

To non-Quakers, the peace testimony of the Religious Society of Friends is probably the best known of our historic testimonies. For many Quakers it is the most important of them, and indeed for some is what uniquely sets us apart from everybody else.

1: "The Quaker testimony concerning war does not set up as its standard of value the attainment of individual or national safety, neither is it based primarily on the iniquity of taking human life, profoundly important as that aspect of the question is. It is based ultimately on the conception of `that of God in every man' to which the Christian in the presence of evil is called to make appeal, following out a line of thought and conduct which, involving suffering as it may do, is, in the long run, the most likely to reach the inward witness and so change the evil mind into the right mind. This result is not achieved by war". *Central and Southern Africa Yearly Meeting, Handbook of Practice and Procedure, What do Quakers believe?*

2: "Jesus' teachings, the whole spirit of the Gospel, and the provisions of his grace urge us to live in peace with all humankind. We encourage our members to find new alternative forms of carrying out civil justice and of working within our society for compensating for insults and errors.

We consider war to be the worst violation of the sacredness of human life, and we confirm our belief that any war is entirely incompatible with Christ's teachings. No argument can be abused for releasing nations and individuals from their obedience to our Lord, who said: 'Love your enemies, bless those who curse you, do good to those who hate you and pray for those who humiliate and pursue you' (*Matthew 5:44*).

It is our intention to 'live in that life and power that takes away the occasion of all war' and suffer violence if it was necessary (as our Lord suffered it), to never return evil for evil - and at the same time fight for non-violent means and methods for bringing about peace through justice between nations or individuals, and for eliminating anything which might provoke war, enmity and hatred among human beings". *Cuba Yearly Meeting, Faith and Practice*

3: "Since all human beings are children of God, Friends are called to love and respect all persons and to overcome evil with good. Friends' peace testimony arises from the power of Christ working in our hearts. Our words and lives should testify to this power and should stand as a positive witness in a world still torn by strife and violence.

The Society of Friends has consistently held that war is contrary to the Spirit of Christ. It stated its position clearly in the Declaration to Charles II in 1660:'*We utterly deny all outward wars and strife, and fightings with outward weapons, for any end, or under any pretense whatsoever; this is our testimony to the whole world.... The Spirit of Christ, by which we are guided, is not changeable, so as once to command us from a thing as evil, and again to move us unto it; and we certainly know, and testify to the world, that the Spirit of Christ, which leads us into all truth, will never move us to fight and war against any man with outward weapons, neither for the Kingdom of Christ nor for the Kingdoms of this world.... Therefore, we cannot learn war any more*'.

Our historic peace testimony must be also a living testimony, as we work to give concrete expression to our ideals, often in opposition to prevailing opinion. We recognize that the peace testimony requires us to honor that of God in every person, and therefore to avoid not only physical violence but also more subtle forms—psychological, economic, or systemic.

In explaining his unwillingness to serve in the army, George Fox records that 'I told them...that I lived in the virtue of that life and power that takes away the occasion of all wars'. When we find that life and power within ourselves, we are strengthened to be valiant for God's truth, to endure the suffering that may befall our lot". *Philadelphia Yearly Meeting, Faith and Practice, Living in the world*

4: "We believe God desires reconciliation with all peoples and between all peoples, having made peace with sinful humanity through His cross. As our gracious salvation has taken away any enmity between God and believers, so also we believe God calls His people to exemplify love in our relationships with each other and the world.

As Jesus did in His own life, we believe that we are called to bear witness to God's love for us and his love for our enemies by suffering for them, if necessary, even unto death. We believe God calls His people to practice peacemaking as a basic element of Christian obedience and discipleship. Violence, in its essence, is evil and inhumane, and contrary to the gospel of love and peace. Consequently, our new life in Christ calls us to rid ourselves of violence in its many and different forms, refusing to use it as a tool for good. With regard to military service we encourage prayerful and conscientious study and obedience to our Lord's call to peacemaking. While each person must live out his or her understanding of Scripture, the time-tested Friends' counsel is to decline to serve, or where the state allows, to give alternative service. In keeping with the teachings and example of Jesus, we are each called to oppose war and violence, to alleviate suffering, to work for reconciliation, and to promote justice in the name of our Lord Jesus Christ and the power of His love. (*Matt. 26:51-54; Luke 6:27-36; Romans 12:14-21; 1 Cor. 6:7; 1 Tim. 2:1-8; 1 Peter 2:19-24; Is. 2:4*)" *Evangelical Friends Church Southwest, Faith and Practice, Fervent Convictions*

5: "All war is against the principles and precepts of our divine Lord Jesus Christ, the Prince of Peace, who teaches us to love our enemies and commands us to put on the spiritual weapons (*Eph 6:10, Gal 5:16-18*)" *East Africa Yearly Meeting North, Faith and Practice, The Statement of Faith*

5: "The teachings of Jesus, the whole spirit of His gospel, and the provisions of His grace call men and women to live at peace with one another. Life is sacred; therefore, war and violence are not consistent with the practice of Christian holiness to which believers are called by Christ. Members are encouraged to find nonviolent methods for achieving civil justice and the reparation of wrongs. (See the *Richmond Declaration of Faith, Section N: Peace*) An alternative to military service is to use the provision of the Selective Service Act in order to perform alternative civilian services.

Jesus taught that we should love one another. He consistently modeled loving actions. Jesus came to serve and to save. He challenges us to do the same.

Violence can take the form of physical or verbal abuse, intimidation, and manipulation. In the home, in our schools and neighborhoods, with family, friends, or strangers, we each choose how we relate and respond to one another. Even in those situations where we believe we are being wronged, Jesus calls us to respond with nonviolent, prayerful methods. must start in the home". *Rocky Mountain Yearly Meeting, Faith and Practice, Faith in Action*

6: "We hold that the supreme duty of every one of us is that he should honestly and prayerfully endeavour to ascertain what God's will for him is, and that, having satisfied himself as to this, he should strive to obey that Will.

While we willingly extend liberty of conscience to those of our members who have felt it right to engage in military service, at the same time we fully maintain our adherence to the principles of Peace which our Religious Society has always held, and our belief that all war is contrary to the precepts and the spirit of the Gospel of our Lord Jesus Christ.". *Ireland Yearly Meeting, Christian Experience*

7: "In the matter of war, as in many other areas, the Christian is caught in a tension between the Scriptural command to 'be subject to the governing authorities' on one hand and the conviction of the other hand that 'we must obey God rather than men'. Even among Friends this has led to differing convictions as to how these commands shall be applied in specific situations. We respect individual conscience and surround our members with loving care whether they for Christ's sake refuse military service or feel obligated to serve in some capacity in armed force.

This liberty is not to be interpreted as any softening of our firm conviction that war is wrong as a method of settling dispute, being unchristian, destructive of our highest values and productive of the seeds of future wars. We therefore as a church, unequivovally support young Friends who as conscientious objectors to war refuse military service. And we are concerned to find alternative solutions based upon justice and rightoeousness for all peoples, and are deeply moved to participate in the new calls to peacemaking which are being sounded in our day". *Philippines Evangelical Friends Church, Statement of Faith and Christian Practice*

Queries for discussion

What does the Quaker peace testimony mean to you?

How do you yourself demonstrate the peace testimony in the world?

Have there been occasions when you have responded to a situation in a violent way, whether physically, verbally or emotionally?

What was the outcome?

Who do you find it most difficult to love as Christ commanded?

Has there been an occasion in your life when you showed love to an adversary and that love bore fruit?

7: Worship

The early Friends' form of worship was based on silence and anybody could be called to vocal ministry by the Holy Spirit. This truly set them apart from the other Christians of their day. Today many Quakers still practice an 'unprogrammed' form of worship. The majority of Friends in the world have a pre-planned Sunday worship service led by a pastor or other worship leader. Either way, Quaker worship is still peculiarly Quaker, tracing its roots back to the earliest meetings for worship which George Fox and his friends participated in.

1: "The Yearly Meeting has a heartfelt concern that our meetings offer a form of worship which is simple, pure, and spiritual. We meet together in silence and strive to free our minds and hearts for the purpose of spiritual worship. We must then wait in humble reverence for the spiritual ability to worship the Lord of Heaven and Earth in a manner acceptable to Him.

As each soul feels a spirit of supplication answered by the quickening influence of the Holy Spirit, we approach the Throne of Grace; that is to say, we are enabled to enter into an attitude of true worship, in gratitude and praise.

Though the nearness to God may result in spoken ministry or vocal prayer, the distinctive excellence of heavenly favor consists in the direct communication with the Heavenly Father by the inward revelation of the Spirit of Christ.

It is urged that Friends encourage their children and others under their care in the habit of regular and orderly attendance at both First-day and other meetings. Such should be taught, in proportion to their understanding, how to wait in stillness upon the Lord, that they, too, may receive their portion of His spiritual favor through the tendering influence of His Holy Spirit.

Drowsiness and habitual tardiness are not necessarily evidence of a negligent attitude toward the living purpose of our meetings for worship, but because they might appear so, both should be avoided as far as possible, lest they become hindrances to others present.

In preparation for meeting, the individual may find that he becomes quiet in expectation, or he may desire to read Scripture or other devotional material as a quieting discipline. Sometimes First-day school, a discussion group, a family meeting or reading is found helpful in this preparation process.

We appoint an hour to meet for worship. The meeting begins in silence, according to the injunction, "Be still and know that I am God" (*Psalms 46:10*). Friends thus allow themselves to become quiet by putting aside words, thoughts of business, cares, and topics of the day.

Not all Friends can become truly quiet instantly or at every meeting. It cannot be done at will; indeed, "will" too often proves an obstacle. After a time, however, a number of worshippers do seem to be sharing the Presence of a guiding Spirit. Vocal ministry or prayer may or may not occur, springing from the heart of one or more worshippers. Any who feel called by an inward urging of the Holy Spirit to speak are advised to do so, simply and clearly.

As the meeting continues, there comes a time when a Friend, chosen beforehand, feels the appropriate time has come to close the meeting, and shakes hands with his nearest neighbor". *Ohio Yearly Meeting (Conservative), Faith and Practice, The Meeting for Worship*

2: "On one never-to-be-forgotten Sunday morning, I found myself one of a small company of silent worshippers who were content to sit down together without words, that each one might feel after and draw near to the Divine Presence, unhindered at least, if not helped, by any human utterance. Utterance I knew was free, should the words be given; and, before the meeting was over, a sentence or two were uttered in great simplicity by an old and apparently untaught man, rising in his place amongst the rest of us. I did not pay much attention to the words he spoke, and I have no recollection of their purport. My whole soul was filled with the unutterable peace of the undisturbed opportunity for communion with God, with the sense that at last I had found a place where I might, without the faintest suspicion of insincerity, join with others in simply seeking His presence. To sit down in silence could at the least pledge me to nothing; it might

open to me (as it did that morning) the very gate of heaven. And, since that day, now more than seventeen years ago, Friends' meetings have indeed been to me the greatest of outward helps to a fuller and fuller entrance into the spirit from which they have sprung; the place of the most soul-subduing, faith-restoring, strengthening, and peaceful communion, in feeding upon the bread of life, that I have ever known". *Britain Yearly Meeting, Quaker Faith and Practice, 2.02*

3: "Worship is a privilege of the Christian. It is a spiritual experience in which believers give themselves to communion and fellowship with the Heavenly Father, a time when they consciously feel and give adoration and love and gratitude to God. It is a time of reverent coming before the Almighty God as a child of His by grace.

The first preparation for profitable worship is a humble spirit which recognizes the grace of God in giving us this privilege. Equally important is a contrite spirit which is submissive to His Lordship and superior will for our daily living. When these attitudes prevail, worship is full of meaning and reward. (*Psalm 51:17*)

Worship may be silent or vocal, taking various forms; it does not depend on certain ceremonies or traditions. Worship is a natural outgrowth of union with Christ and should be directed by His Spirit.

The service of worship will usually include times of prayer, praise, and preaching. During public worship services we should also allow sufficient time for reflection, meditation, and decision. Inasmuch as public worship aids Christians in their growth in grace, is the focal point of the church's local ministry, and is a testimony to the surrounding community of the importance of worshipping God, our members should attend the services of their congregation regularly and faithfully. They should impress upon their children the same religious practice, believing that thus they will aid in leading their children to salvation and to the worship of God.

From the beginning of His earthly life (*Matthew 2:2*) and throughout the ages of time (*Revelation 4:10-11*), the Lord Jesus

Christ has been, is, and will be the object of worship. We make Him the center of our worship and delight in collectively and personally giving Him praise and adoration as God. Without His presence through the Holy Spirit our worship would have neither meaning nor depth.

Believers are committed to the work of God, not only to manifest personal righteousness as the fruit of a new life, but also to share their faith. All Christians are called upon to witness by word and deed, in Christlikeness demonstrating love, forgiveness, and the way of peace. Certain ones are called and ordained by God for a special service of leadership in His Church; their service may be that of teaching, evangelizing, pastoring, or administration. The church should recognize such special gifts among its members and encourage their use". *Evangelical Friends Church – Mid-America Yearly Meeting, Faith and Practice, Testimonies Regarding Sacred Worship*

4: "The Meeting for Worship is set apart for corporate aspiration. Its basis is silent and direct communion with God. It affords opportunity for a resolute fixing of the heart and mind upon that which is unchangeable and eternal, making it a time of expectant waiting for the leading of the Divine Spirit.

Gathering in an outward silence is not enough. Each individual must consciously and earnestly seek in humble reverence for a renewed sense of the inward power of the Spirit. From the depths of that stillness comes the consciousness of the presence of God. In this experience individuals will not only find direction for their lives and strength for their needs, but will also feel an urge to share with others the thoughts and aspirations that have come to them. As the worshipers seek to be led to larger visions and pray to become more obedient to the Christ within, their united effort will release to all in the Meeting the riches of the Spirit.

True worship, whether vocal or silent, is offering ourselves, body, mind, and soul, for the doing of God's will. During the silent waiting, the flow of the Divine Spirit from heart to heart is often felt. 'One is your teacher, and all ye are brethren'. Worshipers should gather in a spirit of silent prayer with a willingness to give, as well as receive, so that the full possibilities of the Meeting hour can be reached and its influence extended throughout the community from week to week". *Ohio Valley Yearly Meeting, Book of Discipline, Religious Expression*

5: "Worship is the adoring response of heart and mind to the Spirit of God. The meeting for worship brings a personal and corporate renewal, an edification and communion of believers, and a witness of the Gospel to the unconverted. We recognize the value of silence to center our thoughts upon God. We believe the Spirit speaks to worshipers through persons He has prepared and selected, whose message may be given in various modes by men or women, children or adults. We believe God calls some persons to a special preaching ministry, which the church should respectfully receive. Friends observe the first day of the week for corporate worship and for rest". *Northwest Yearly Meeting, Faith and Practice, Friends Faith – What Friends Believe*

6: "The meeting for worship is the heart of every Friends' Meeting. It is based on faith that men and women can enter into direct communion with God.

In the excitement of their discovery that Christ was alive and had "come to teach His people Himself," early Friends gathered for worship fully expecting the Spirit to be present, and out of their hushed expectancy they entered into a fellowship with God that changed their lives. In the course of such worship came new revelations of Truth and a force that drove Friends out into the world to spread the news and to serve humanity.

Friends in New England try in their meetings for worship to capture the same spirit, a sense of God's presence in the midst, and to be open to new revelation. Some New England Friends gather in silent waiting upon God without designated leadership or program. Some are led in worship by a pastor whose function is to encourage and cultivate the ministry of each individual. In either case, for the meeting to be successful, all must share and respond.

Preparation for worship is essential. Preparation is a continual process of prayer, of reading the Bible and other religious literature, of learning from human experiences, and of daily practicing the presence of God. Some come on Sunday morning expecting to receive God's revelation with no previous effort on their part. For the cup to overflow on Sunday, however, it must be filled up all through the week. Early Friends came to worship with their cup overflowing, and it was then that the power was given to go out and to share the Truth that had come to them.

In the unprogrammed meeting, as the worship proceeds, out of communion with God a message may come to one of the worshipping individuals. Sometimes the message is purely personal; at other times it seems to belong to the meeting. The worshipper is then under divine compulsion to share it with fellow seekers, to contribute to the vocal service of the meeting, however haltingly.

In the meetings with pastoral leadership, the pastor may prepare a message and an order of service during the week, but the pastor is only a worshipper among worshippers, and the life of the pastoral worship depends on the response of the group. Ideally the prepared message arises not just from the pastor's own spiritual resources, but from the worship of the group.

Not all meetings, whether pastoral or based on silence, achieve a high level. Yet God does break through the crust of apathy, of worldly preoccupations or lack of preparation. We are humble learners in the school of Christ, and our weaknesses and failures should not deter us. When a meeting for worship gathers in active expectancy of God's presence with complete openness of heart and mind, the power to change lives will arise". *New England Yearly Meeting, Faith and Practice, The Meeting for Worship*

7: "Worship neither depends on forms nor on their total absence; it can be with or without words. Both silence and vocal exercises are recognized and appreciated, not as aims, but as the means of achieving an aim, which is the divine blessing of the individual and the congregation As Master of the Assembly, the Lord leads and guides the exercises that are advantageous for his congregation. He calls us to be and qualifies us as his messengers, and each believer must be ready to obey his will". *Cuba Yearly Meeting, Faith and Practice*

Queries for discussion

Do you always find meeting for worship to be a deeply spiritual period?

Can you see the spiritual in the mundane?

Have you experienced Friends' worship authentically in a tradition other than your own?

Have you tried to lead worship outside your own usual tradition?

How do you feel programmed Friends' worship differs from any other Christian church service?

What separates an unprogrammed Quaker meeting for worship from a prayer or meditation circle?

Have you ever felt you might have 'come to meeting as you went from it and gone from it as you came to it'?

What ways of worship can you conceive of outside of the normal practices of Quakers?

Can you recall a time when you particularly felt God's presence in worship?

What were the main characteristics of that occasion?

8: Jesus Christ

Quakers worldwide hold to differing views about Jesus Christ. Even within yearly meeting's individual Friends hold a wide perspective on the place and nature of Jesus. For George Fox, Jesus was a very real person who he felt he had met as personally as the apostle Paul did on the road to Damascus. Without the person of Jesus there is no doubt there would be no Religious Society of Friends.

1: "Jesus Christ, the only begotten Son of God, is the second person of the Trinity and is God's revelation of Himself to the world. He was divine and yet human, being conceived by God's Spirit and born of a virgin. Through the blood He shed dying on the cross, Jesus Christ became the atonement for sin, thus providing direct access to God by His priesthood. Upon His resurrection from the dead, He ascended again to the right hand of His Father, assuming the role of Intercessor and drawing people to God by His Spirit. When Jesus Christ returns to earth, He will receive His Church and judge the world". *Evangelical Friends Church – Mid America Yearly Meeting, Faith and Practice, Basic Beliefs (Jesus Christ)*

2: "Since Friends believe that the Spirit is actively present among them as teacher, they have always trusted in it to reveal the truth to individuals insofar as they are prepared to receive it. And while Friends do uphold certain principles and beliefs as a corporate body, they do not require adoption or adherence to these as a condition of membership. They do expect that each person be true to his or her own spiritual experience. Friends' beliefs, traditions, and teachings are meant to be testimonies to help individuals discern the leadings of the Inward Teacher in the midst of worldly voices that vie for allegiance.

Friends' expression of their encounters with God have traditionally been grounded in religious experience rather than in doctrine. These experiences have led Friends to use traditional Christian language in fresh ways: 'Christ', then, may refer to the historical Jesus or to the Inward Teacher who enters their lives to lead them toward oneness with God; 'the Holy Spirit' may become the loving activity of God within each person's life and the life of the meeting; 'the Word of God' can be heard through the Bible and through the direct expression of the Spirit. Friends strive to listen to 'that which is eternal', seeking to come together 'at a place deeper than words'". *Southern Appalachian Yearly Meeting and Association, Faith and Practice, The religious tradition of Friends*

3: "We are called to share with others our experience that God is actively present in the world and in every human heart and may be encountered by those who turn to God in openness and expectation. The Religious Society of Friends is a fellowship of persons who have this faith, and we invite those who have not found a spiritual home to enter into our fellowship. We know that words alone cannot witness to these truths. When our lives speak, when they reflect an enthusiastic, contagious appreciation of Jesus and his teachings, our words of witness will bear convincing authority". *New York Yearly Meeting, Faith and Practice, Fruits of the Spirit - Publishing the Truth: Outreach*

4: "Have faith in God. How simple it sounds! Yet how difficult for those wracked by pain, of tortured mind; and how difficult for the lonely, the starving, the homeless and the hopeless. How difficult, too, for honest searchers after truth when the collective faith seems to be disintegrating. Yet Jesus was as simple as that. His simplicity confounded the intellectuals of His day; the simplicity of the early Christians confounded the sophistry of the Greeks, and the simplicity of the Quakers confounded the theologians of the 17th century. As a new Yearly Meeting we enter into a new phase of our life as a Quaker community in New Zealand and we face a very different religious and secular atmosphere than did the early Christians or the early Friends. For the early Friends the Word of God was not only the Word spoken through the prophets and by Jesus himself, it was the Eternal Word made flesh and therefore intelligible to man in terms of human life in the person of Jesus. More than that, it was the authentic Word of God recreated again and again in the personal life of men and women who wait upon God for the renewal of their spirits and the revealing of further light.

We need to take a fresh look at the faith of our fathers and in the language of Paul: 'Put all things to the test and hold fast to that which is good'". *Aotearoa New Zealand Yearly Meeting, Faith and Practice, 4.06*

5: "As the inward experience of communion with God is central to our life and worship, so are spoken testimonies of invaluable service to the meeting. Such sharing is but the beginning of our duty to the whole of society. This is a distinctive, yet not exclusive, service of Gospel Ministry. As Friends, we are persuaded that true Gospel Ministry comes not of man, but through him by direct revelation from Jesus Christ by the prompting and guidance of the Holy Spirit. Nonetheless, some meetings, entirely silent, give ample evidence of deep spiritual life.

The essential qualification for the ministry is the direct preparation by God himself in those individuals who are called to the service. As the gift is Divine, so the service should be freely and faithfully discharged without any view of reward from man. The express command of Christ, our head and high priest, was 'Freely ye have received, freely give'". *Ohio Yearly Meeting (Conservative), The Book of Discipline, Ministry of the Gospel*

6: "By humbly giving thanks we would like to bear loyal testimony to our Lord's eternal power and rule in his Church. Thanks to him the redeemed of all generations have received the light, forgiveness and joy. All members of this Church, whichever name and denomination they carry, are those who have been baptised by one same Spirit in one same Body; who are living stones, built upon Christ Jesus, the Eternal Foundation, and who are united in faith, love and fraternity, within and by the Father and the Son. Of this Church Jesus the Lord is the sole head, and all its members are united within him". *Cuba Yearly Meeting, Faith and Practice*

7: "To me, being a Christian is a particular way of life, not the unquestioning acceptance of a particular system of theology, not belief in the literal truth of the Virgin birth, or the Resurrection and Ascension, but being the kind of person that Jesus wanted his followers to be and doing the things he told them to do...

Nor, it seems to me, can you live a Christian life unless, like Jesus, you believe in the power of goodness, of justice, of mercy and of love; unless you believe in these so strongly that you are prepared to put them to the acid test of experiment; unless these constitute the real meaning of life for you, more important than life itself, as they were for Jesus". *Britain Yearly Meeting, Quaker Faith and Practice, 20.26*

8: "We believe in the bodily resurrection of Jesus Christ, in His ascension into Heaven and in the bodily resurrection of both the saved and the lost; they that are saved into the resurrection of eternal life, and they that are lost into the resurrection of eternal death and punishment. We believe in the bodily return, that is, the second coming of our Lord Jesus Christ in great power and glory to judge the living and the dead". *East Africa Yearly Meeting North, Faith and Practice, The Statement of Faith*

Queries for discussion

How does Jesus affect you in your everyday life?

Is he your Lord and Saviour?

How do you feel about Friends who have a different experience to you of their encounter with Jesus?

Do you hold to the example Jesus set in his teachings when you meet Friends with a different perspective?

What do you think is Jesus' most important teaching?

How do you perceive Jesus alive and active in the world today?

If the man Jesus was to appear before you right now, how might you address him?

9: Truth

The name of the Religious Society of Friends stems from one of the earliest names George Fox and his followers were known by, the *Friends of Truth*. The testimony to truth predates the peace testimony, and encompasses not only the Quaker witness to Truth in the spiritual sense, but also includes a witness to personal integrity and honesty. It also means to be 'true to oneself', following the promptings of the Holy Spirit in our own hearts.

1: "We believe our ability to communicate with one another was given to us by God. As our Maker, He is the creator of speech and language. This gift, like every other gift from God, is to be guarded and used wisely. Friends have a testimony about how we are to speak. Following Jesus' command, Friends decline to use oaths of any kind, even in legal settings, preferring to use a simple affirmation (*Matthew 5:33-37; James 5:12*). In earlier times, Friends refused to use the second person plural, 'you', to address an individual of higher rank or social status, using instead the singular forms, 'thee' or 'thou' to address all individuals.

At the heart of this testimony was a belief that language was given to us to communicate truth. Taking an oath implied that somehow one's other words were not always as true, an abasement of language and an implied dishonesty. Formal address required bowing to a social convention based on a passing human reality, and not on the eternal values of the Kingdom of God.

We believe the Lord is calling us to redeem our speech. Words were given to us to tell the truth. We should be very aware of the constant temptation to exchange clarity for what presents best, and simplicity of speech for calculated expressions. When we disagree, we can and should express ourselves clearly and honestly, but we must be careful not to dishonor those with whom we disagree. Most of all, we must embrace the positive use of words. The Scriptures command us to bless, encourage, and honor each other. More than avoiding the misuse of words, the Lord is calling us to put speech to work for the gracious and beneficial purposes for which He created it". *Evangelical Friends Church Southwest, Faith and Practice, Fervent Convictions*

3: "The testimony of integrity calls us to wholeness; it is the whole of life open to Truth. When lives are centered in the Spirit, beliefs and actions are congruent, and words are dependable. As we achieve wholeness in ourselves, we are better able to heal the conflict and fragmentation in our community and in the world.

Integrity is a demanding discipline. We are challenged by cultural values and pressures to conform. Integrity requires that we be fully responsible for our actions. Living with integrity requires living a life of reflection, living in consistency with our beliefs and testimonies, and doing so regardless of personal consequences. Not least, it calls for a single standard of truth. From the beginning, Friends have held to this standard, and have often witnessed against the mainstream. When they suffered in consequence of their witness against secular order, their integration of belief and practice upheld them in adversity.

Speaking the truth in all circumstances and at all times, as enjoined in the Bible, is shown in the refusal to take oaths. Oaths imply that there are times the truth is not necessarily told and early Friends believed that the system of requiring oaths taught people that lies were otherwise acceptable. Truth telling led to a one-price system in merchandising, with fair value for fair price rather than bargaining or discrimination between buyers.

Friends believe in speaking simply, avoiding misleading words or emotionally manipulative language, which could divert from the discernment of God's will. Commitment to truth requires authenticity and veracity in following one's conscience, illuminated by the Inner Light. When we depart from truth, we separate ourselves from God. Integrity is not simply a habit of speech, but a way of life increasingly aligned with God's will". *Pacific Yearly Meeting, Faith and Practice, Living Our Faith*

4: "The Quaker testimony to truthfulness is central to the practice of its faith by members of the Religious Society of Friends. From the beginning Friends have believed that they could have direct and immediate communication with God which would enable them to discern right ethical choices. They soon experienced common leadings of the Spirit which became formalised into testimonies...

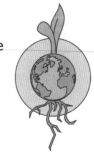

Arising from the teaching of Jesus as related in the writings of John and James: `Let your yes mean yes and your no mean no', Quakers perceived that with a conscience illuminated by the Light, life became an integrated whole with honesty as its basis.

From time to time ... adherence to factual truth can give rise to profound dilemmas for Quaker Peace and Social Witness workers if they are in possession of information which could be used to endanger people's lives or give rise to the abuse of fundamental human rights... Some of us are clear that in certain difficult circumstances we may still uphold our testimony to truthfulness while at the same time declining to disclose confidences which we have properly accepted. Such withholding of the whole truth is not an option to be undertaken lightly as a convenient way out of a dilemma. We all accept that ultimately it is up to an individual's own conscience, held in the Light, to decide how to respond". *Britain Yearly Meeting, Quaker Faith and Practice, 20.45*

5: "Historic testimonies of the Society of Friends against taking oaths, joining secret organizations, gambling and using addictive substances grew out of efforts of Friends to live with integrity and consistency. To swear an oath implied that one is obliged to be truthful only under oath. Joining secret organizations, gambling and using addictive and/or consciousness altering substances were recognized as practices which diverted resources from useful purposes, distracted attention from the Inner Light, and placed obstacles in the way of Friends seeking to lead lives of integrity. We recognize the spirit of these testimonies and endeavor to apply the same principles in our lives today.

Honesty and simplicity are essential parts of personal responsibility. We manifest our commitment to Truth in all we do. We can have joy and beauty in our lives without allowing material things to dominate them. We need to free ourselves from distractions that interfere with our search for inner peace, and accept with thanksgiving all that promotes fullness and aids in service to the divine Center". *Iowa Yearly Meeting (Conservative), Advices and Queries, 8: Personal Responsibility*

6: "Work is part of a full life and can be a means of self-expression. When done with others, it fosters community. It provides the necessities of living.

Coming to a consciousness of the spiritual nature of our work can be a slow process, but many forms of work can be honorable if we approach them with integrity, diligence, and concern. The workplace, whether ideal or not, enables us to put into action conflict negotiation, mediation, centering, listening, silence, and love. In fact, in the marketplace our strengths may be most tested, and our faithfulness most treasured.

All of the business relationships of Friends should be carried on in a spirit of love and service. If we keep before us the faith that there is an indwelling Spirit in every person we encounter, then personal dealings and relations of management and labor become integral to our religious lives and allow us to witness to our testimonies. Work can be an opportunity for personal ministry, and many Friends try to choose paid and voluntary work that furthers justice, freedom, and equality and that helps to remove the seeds of war and conflict". *New York Yearly Meeting, Faith and Practice, Fruits of the Spirit - Work*

Queries for discussion

Can you conceive of instances where the greater Truth is served better by the withholding of another truth?

Have you been in such a situation yourself?

What course did you take?

With the benefit of hindsight, was that the best course?

Do you lead a life whereby maintaining truth and integrity comes relatively easy, or is your situation such that it can be a challenging effort to maintain these principles?

Do you think the testimony against the swearing of oaths in a court still has deep spiritual meaning today in your country?

What do you think could be an equivalent witness for today's world?

10: Equality

Perhaps the most challenging aspect of the early Quaker witness was the testimony to equality. At that time the world was riddled with hierarchies, and even failing to remove one's hat to a supposed social superior could result in a beating, a prison sentence, or worse. Friends' consistent acting out their belief that all are equal under God is as relevant in the world today as it was in England in 1647

1: "The Quaker principle of group action is called consensus or harmony. By harmony is meant the pacifist technique of allowing unity to emerge without coercion, on an individual basis, whether this be in the meeting or on a worldwide scale. Friends believe that only by thus allowing all to participate in social processes can true community be reached.

This mode of decision-making is grounded in Friends' experience of spiritual unity in the Inner Light. The appeal to the Inner Light as a source of unity does not imply victory of one person or party over another, but the victory of love and truth which are often on the side of the weak.

While Friends know from their own experience how difficult it is to maintain a spirit of love and openness to the ideas of others, they believe that any superficial unity attained merely by power or by force of the majority is worthless, since true unity is a deep conviction of spiritual oneness underlying agreement on issues and actions.

Just as Friends find all individuals to be at one in the Light, so are all found potentially equal in moral and spiritual stature by virtue of the universality of the Light. Friends testimony to social equality grows out of this awareness. Friends believe that equality of spiritual opportunities involves a demand for equal opportunity in all areas of our social, cultural, legal, political, and economic life". *North Carolina Yearly Meeting (Conservative), Faith and Practice, Doctrine and Testimonies – III: Harmony*

2: "Harsh political oppression from 1948 until 1994 was designed to prevent community and neighbourliness. The Meeting tried to be 'colour blind'. Many hours were spent agonising over letters of protest and advise the oppressive government. Many hours were spent travelling by day and night, over the no-mans-land between Johannesburg and Soweto. Individual friends worked through a wide range of organisations, to alleviate, protest and remove Apartheid. We were active in the work of the South African Council of Churches. Some found the South African situation intolerable and emigrated. Others tenaciously stayed to do what they could to remove the dark cloud of Apartheid.

The meeting as a whole remained true to Quaker principles of equality, justice, and 'walking cheerfully over the earth answering that of God in everyone'. Many individual friends have testified that without this spiritual support and nurturing their creative activity in the community would have been impossible. Because Johannesburg had the only international airport, the meeting was blessed by a 'heavenly host' of foreign visitors, who worshipped, talked, encouraged and corresponded with us. Visiting wardens of the meeting house were a source of quiet support and great encouragement. The contribution of every person who has been associated with the meeting is valued.

Since 1994 the Meeting has continued to nurture those who wrestle to follow their Inner Light in building community. Opportunities for discovering a wide variety of new and valuable roles are greater than ever". *Central and Southern Africa Yearly Meeting, Handbook of Practice and Procedure, History of the Quakers in Southern Africa*

3: "Friends believe that all people have the capacity to bear and respond to the Light and that all forms of human relations should reflect this spiritual truth. Deeply concerned that every individual, as a beloved child of God, be respected and afforded equal access to social opportunities, Friends believed that we are called to work toward an end to prejudice and oppression.

Each of us has God-given gifts that express themselves in different ways. Friends believe that the way in which God's gifts are realized may be shaped by the world in which we live. Our ability to both bear and respond to the Light can be affected by social prejudices that dim awareness of God's leadings.

A commitment to equality, the first of Friends social testimonies, led early Friends to affirm that no person is superior to another because of birth, wealth, or formal education. They rejected the use of honorific titles, provided expanded leadership roles for women in their communities, and eschewed 'hat honor', removing one's hat as a sign of deference. They retained the traditional 'thee' and 'thou' to avoid the emerging seventeenth century usage of granting an undue distinction to an individual with a plural 'you'. Modern Friends have expanded our awareness of what equality demands, in its continued application in our daily lives.

In seeking to apply this testimony, Friends have often been in the forefront of social change. Recognition of inherent worth in all people despite individual or group differences has often caused Friends to live and act contrary to accepted societal norms, rejecting stereotyping, discrimination, and artificial barriers that separate people from one another. Equality has been the foundation of Friends approach to each other and the world.

We believe all are equally empowered by God and encourage all to speak for themselves, expressing their own experiences and goals. We must speak the truth to others as it is revealed to us, and we must listen for truth that is in them, lest we miss it. Understanding other's perspectives can change us and inform the actions we take to work toward equality. In our continuing spiritual search, we are open to revising our approach to social change as new insights arise.

We seek a world free of oppression, where laws and customs foster human dignity. We encourage all people to realize their full potential as human beings bearing the light of God". *Southern Appalachian Yearly Meeting and Association, Faith and Practice, Testifying to the Life of the Spirit: Equality*

4: "We are part of an economic system characterized by inequality and exploitation. Such a society is defended and perpetuated by entrenched power.

Friends can help relieve social and economic oppression and injustice by first seeking spiritual guidance in our own lives. We envision a system of social and economic justice that ensures the right of every individual to be loved and cared for; to receive a sound education; to find useful employment; to receive appropriate health care; to secure adequate housing; to obtain redress through the legal system; and to live and die in dignity. Friends maintain historic concern for the fair and humane treatment of persons in penal and mental institutions.

Wide disparities in economic and social conditions exist among groups in our society and among nations of the world. While most of us are able to be responsible for our own economic circumstances, we must not overlook the effects of unequal opportunities among people. Friends' belief in the Divine within everyone leads us to support institutions which meet human needs and to seek to change institutions which fail to meet human needs. We strengthen community when we work with others to help promote justice for all". *Iowa Yearly Meeting (Conservative), Advices and Queries, 11: Social and economic responsibility*

5: "'There is neither Jew nor Greek, slave nor free, male nor female, for you are all one in Christ Jesus'. *(Galatians 3:28, The New Jerusalem Bible)*

Friends testimony on equality is rooted in the holy expectation that there is that of God in everyone, including adversaries and people from widely different stations, life experiences, and religious persuasions. All must therefore be treated with integrity and respect. The conviction that each person is equally a child of God opened the way for women to be leaders in the Religious Society of Friends: both women and men ministered in Friends Meetings from earliest days.

The testimony of equality does not imply that all individuals in a particular role are the same; it recognizes that the same measure of God's grace is available to everyone. John Woolman exemplified this belief in his travel among Native Americans:

'Love was the first motion, and thence a concern arose to spend some time with the Indians, that I might feel and understand their life and the spirit they live in, if haply I might receive some instruction from them, or they be in any degree helped forward by my following the leadings of Truth amongst them'. *(John Woolman, Journal, 1763, ed J. G. Whittier, 1871, p192)*

Before Friends became pacifists, they were dismissed from the army for refusing to treat officers as superior. George Fox and other early Friends demonstrated their conviction that all persons were of equal worth by refusing to take off their hats to those who claimed higher rank, and by addressing everyone with the singular 'thou' (or 'thee' in America) rather than the honorific plural 'you'.

Friends recognize that unjust inequities persist throughout society, and that difficult work remains to rid ourselves and the Religious Society of Friends from prejudice and inequitable treatment based upon gender, class, race, age, sexual orientation, physical attributes, or other categorizations. Both in the public realm - where Friends may 'speak truth to power' - and in intimate familial contexts, Friends' principles require witness against injustice and inequality wherever it exists". *Pacific Yearly Meeting, Faith and Practice, Testimonies*

Queries for discussion

What does equality mean to you?

How does God call you to witness to the equality of all people?

Are there any areas in which you think Friends corporately or individually fail to live up to the testimony to equality?

What inequalities do you personally see during the course of your daily life?

How does your meeting answer injustice in society around you?

How do you interpret the phrase 'all people are equal' alongside the Biblical idea of 'one body, many parts'?

What do you understand by Jesus' call to 'love one another as I have loved you'?

11: The World Family of Friends

Even in our modern age of instant global communication, Friends today are often surprised to learn that Quakers in other parts of the world think and believe different things to themselves, and worship in a manner they might find alien. Indeed, some Friends are even surprised to learn there are Quakers in certain other parts of the world at all...

1: "We should be prepared to receive someone sent by another Quaker meeting with as much care as we send someone to travel in the ministry.

It is not enough to send foreign Friends into small groups of Friends who will listen politely to their visitors: they should first know their visitors' culture and tradition in order to receive them with open minds and hearts. Friends in London Yearly Meeting need to discover where they stand individually. As we often do not know the personal theologies of members of our own meetings, how can we prepare our own Friends to listen to others? Yet we must. If Friends worldwide are to be a world family of Friends, we have to learn to hear and to understand each other". *Britain Yearly Meeting, Quaker Faith and Practice, 13.26*

2: "National pastors conferences have brought together American ministers from both Friends United Meeting and Evangelical Friends (Alliance) International/NA Region. Various regional and world youth gatherings have strengthened Quaker identity. The All-Friends Conference at St. Louis in 1970 became a catalyst for renewal. The subsequent Faith and Life movement, with its various conferences and study materials, has had similar results. The publications and visiting ministry of the New Foundation movement has also brought spiritual renewal, especially to nonpastoral Friends. The Friends Educational Council and the Friends Association of Higher Education have facilitated spiritual concern for Friends schools. The Friends World Committee for Consultation, begun in 1937, has been used increasingly in recent years by the various yearly meetings for exchanging information and effecting dialogue. Its regional conferences, such as the Conference of Friends in the Americas in 1977, and its periodic world conferences have enhanced mutual understanding,

clarified differences, reduced provincialism, deepened spirituality, and opened the way for a more global witness". *Northwest Yearly Meeting, Faith and Practice, Friends in the World Today*

3: "Central and Southern Africa Yearly Meeting is one of the Yearly Meetings that belongs to the Friends World Committee for Consultation (FWCC).

FWCC is a committee comprising representatives of Yearly Meetings and other Quaker groups throughout the world 'to act in a consultative capacity to promote better understanding among Friends the world over, particularly by the encouragement of joint conferences and intervisitation, the collection and circulation of information about Quaker literature and other activities directed toward that better understanding'.

Nearly all yearly meetings in the world are affiliated to FWCC. Each affiliated Yearly Meeting appoints representatives who are responsible for transacting the business. The number of representatives is based on the size of the yearly meeting. [...]

The FWCC Triennial is a committee meeting which is attended by the current representatives of all Yearly Meetings, plus co-opted members. It meets every three years 'to review what has been done in our name and consider future tasks and programs'.

FWCC expects that its representatives should:

• be committed to openness and to learning from Quakers of other traditions of worship, theology, language and culture

• have wide and deep knowledge of their own Yearly Meetings and their concerns, coupled with firmly-rooted local Quaker commitment

• be in a position to attend all FWCC regional, section and triennial meetings

• look for ways to share their experience of the wider body of Friends within their local and Yearly Meetings, reporting fully and regularly on FWCC meetings and affairs [...]

Open gatherings, called 'World Conferences' of Quakers are held occasionally, 'From time to time the Triennial may be asked to consider whether a World Conference should be held permitting a wider participation and more time for reflection and sharing'". *Central and Southern Africa Yearly Meeting, Handbook of Practice and Procedure, FWCC and CandSAYM*

5: "European Friends tended to follow the liberal drift. The Friends World Committee for Consultation seeks to maintain consultative functions among Friends around the world, but doctrinal differences prevent true unity. The younger churches in Latin America and Africa, the fruit of missionary movements, suffer less from the erosion of belief apparent in the mother church. They continue to lead the Friends Church in growth.

Recent scholarship has focused attention upon the evangelical nature of our early movement. Two of the Yearly Meetings which withdrew from Five Years Meeting in the early 1900s formed a new evangelical alliance in the early 1960s, along with Rocky Mountain Yearly Meeting and Northwest Yearly Meeting. This organization, Evangelical Friends International, is a worldwide movement with regions in North America, Africa, Asia, and Latin America. This Christ-centered movement works hand in hand with Evangelical Friends Mission planting churches and carrying the gospel message around the world to participate in the fulfillment of the Great Commission *(Matthew 28:19-20)*.

Friends United Meeting (formerly the Five Years Meeting) is also a worldwide movement which seeks to be Christ-centered in its work around the world". *Rocky Mountain Yearly Meeting, Faith and Practice, Friends Worlwide*

6: "The First World War was a time of awakening for many Quakers and also a time of testing. In some Meetings, there was little of the peace testimony to be found. Among the Conservative Friends, however, there was generally strong support of the peace testimony as taught by early Friends. Under the leadership of Rufus Jones, representatives from most groups of Quakers joined with other concerned people to form the American Friends Service Committee, a united effort to give relief in Europe to those who were the victims of war and to provide an opportunity for young conscientious objectors to engage in practical programs

for human betterment rather than to participate in war.

A trend toward unity among Friends has been encouraged by a series of Friends World Conferences, and these Conferences have now become an established part of the life of Quakers all over the world. A further development from this has been the birth and growth of the Friends World Committee for Consultation, with the American Section of that Committee providing help and guidance in the United States for many new Meetings and for the unification of Friends' efforts". *Iowa Yearly Meeting (Conservative), Discipline, Summary of Quaker History*

Queries for discussion

What aspect of your own Quaker tradition do you think has particularly kept well the ideals of the earliest Friends?

What aspect of another Quaker tradition do you think the ideals of the early Friends' have been lost?

Is there something about that tradition you feel has kept the original Quaker ideals alive better than your own has?

12: The rich variety of humanity

The Religious Society of Friends has been likened to a prism through which the divine light passes, to become visible in a spectrum of many colours; in this respect, the variety of Quakerism throughout the world is an echo of the variety of the human race itself.

1: "I suppose you all have read that little poem that tells of six blind men of Hindustan who inspected an elephant and decided that it was wholly like the portion that each one happened to feel and not one would listen to the opinion of another. In one way those six blind men were right. We cannot follow the truth as it appears to another. We must follow the road that seems to each of us individually to be the right path. What we must remember is that our road is not the only one that will lead all people to God. Let us help each other as far as possible, but at the same time remember the words 'Judge not, that ye be not judged'".
Aotearoa New Zealand Yearly Meeting, Quaker Faith and Practice, 5.15

2: "'The first of all the commandments is, Hear, O Israel; The Lord our God is one Lord: And thou shalt love the Lord thy God with all thy heart, and with all thy soul, and with all thy mind, and with all thy strength: this is the first commandment. And the second is like, namely this, Thou shalt love thy neighbor as thyself. There is none other commandment greater than these'. *(Mark 12.29-31 (KJV))*

We participate through God in a unity that we did not create and cannot annul. To the question, 'But who is my neighbor?' Jesus replied with the parable of the good Samaritan *(Luke 10)*. Jesus welcomed into his kingdom those who could see in the unfortunate of the world his own presence. 'For when I was hungry, you gave me food; when thirsty, you gave me drink; when I was a stranger you took me into your home, when naked you clothed me; when I was ill you came to my help, when in prison you visited me'. *(Matthew 25.35-6 NEB)*.

Our attempt to treat all other persons with respect, integrity, and love informs our practice and concerns in all our lives, from close interpersonal relationships to the conduct of meetings for business, to the search for international peace. It may be that we shall find unity in Jesus's simple admonition to 'Love one another as I have loved you'. *(John 13.34 KJV)'. New York Yearly Meeting, Faith and Practice, Witness*

3: "Friends place much importance on living our lives in such a way that we will 'come to walk cheerfully over the world answering that of God in everyone'. Our strength lies in the inclusive nature of this phrase: it encompasses children, women and men, people of other faiths and denominations, the secular community, refugees, asylum seekers and the 'more than human' world. We remind ourselves that it includes those on all sides of all conflicts and national leaders who shame us.

In a session on facing our own racism we read, 'This work of the heart is essential to living out our Quaker testimony of equality – the deep moral recognition that we are all equal in the Spirit. It is work we must do'. When we find space for the heart, our work for peace and reconciliation has begun. We believe that every human being is entitled to a space in the world which enhances their dignity". *Australia Yearly Meeting, this we can say, 5.75*

4: "Friends reaffirm the belief that all people are children of one heavenly Father. The Light which leads to unity in the meeting community illuminates all relationships between people everywhere. This Light has led friends into deep concern for Indians, black people and other minority groups who have been victims of prejudice and exploitation. It has inspired work for prisoners and the mentally ill, and has stirred action for the alleviation of poverty and unemployment. It has created testimony for peaceful ways to resolve human conflicts.

As George Fox said in his exhortation to Friends in the ministry: 'Be patterns, be examples in all countries, places, islands, nations, wherever you come; that your carriage and life may preach among all sorts of people, and to them; then you will come to walk cheerfully over the world, answering to that of God in every one; whereby in them ye may be a blessing, and make the witness of God in them to bless you'. *(Journal of George Fox)*

This concept of inclusive brotherhood applies not only to nations and to groups; it makes us realize that we are called to think of everyone as an individual, to deal with each as a child of God. To Jesus every person, even though a harlot, a thief or one of the despised Samaritans, was of infinite worth and might be drawn by love to attain fullness of life as a child of God. Much misunderstanding stems from the tendency to think and talk of nations, racial and religious groups as solid blocks and to forget the varied and precious individuals of whom they are composed". *Iowa Yearly Meeting (Conservative), Discipline, Peace and Social Concerns – Human Brotherhood*

5: "We believe the Christian life is characterized by disciplined devotion and commitment, by a hunger for God and a thirst for righteousness. This commitment is strengthened by habits of prayer and Bible reading. For us this Christian faith involves commitment to the work of Friends. Although we respect freedom of conscience and honor diversity in the family of God, we affirm our covenant with God as Friends people. Therefore, we aim to be faithful to those structures of our denominational life through which our Gospel witness is made clear". *Northwest Yearly Meeting, Faith and Practice, What Friends Believe*

6: "How can we make the meeting a community in which each person is accepted and nurtured, and strangers are welcome? Seek to know one another in the things which are eternal, bear the burden of each other's failings and pray for one another. As we enter with tender sympathy into the joys and sorrows of each other's lives, ready to give help and to receive it, our meeting can be a channel for God's love and forgiveness". *Britain Yearly Meeting, Advices and Queries, 18*

Queries for discussion

Who is your neighbour, in the context of the parable of the good Samaritan?

Are there still some neighbours you would find it particularly difficult to feed, clothe, and give a bed for the night as the good Samaritan did?

From your reading and studying, have you been able to see any common areas which might unite Friends around the world?

Do you feel you have discerned how Christ our present teacher, however you might understand that, has guided you to facilitate understanding within our Quaker family?

Have you been sufficiently humble in asking for guidance, and are you yourself truly open to the possibility of transformation?

What specific areas do you acknowledge you still need extra help to bring yourself under God's light?

How can your meeting community help you grow stronger in God, and how can you help your fellow Quakers to also?

How do you feel God's light especially shines through you?

Epistle from the 1985 World Gathering of Young Friends

Over 300 young Friends from 34 countries, 57 yearly meetings, and 8 monthly meetings under the care of Friends World Committee for Consultation, met at Guilford College, Greensboro, North Carolina in July 1985, to envisage the future of the Religious Society of Friends and to see how their lives should speak within that vision.

We have come together from every continent, separated by language, race, culture, ways we worship God, and beliefs about Christ and God... We have been challenged, shaken up, at times even enraged, intimidated, and offended by these differences in each other. We have grown from this struggle and have felt the Holy Spirit in programmed worship, singing, Bible study, open times of worship and sharing, and silent waiting upon God.

Our differences are our richness, but also our problem. One of our key differences is the different names we give our Inward Teacher. Some of us name that Teacher Lord; others of us use the names Spirit, Inner Light, Inward Christ or Jesus Christ. It is important to acknowledge that these names involve more than language; they involve basic differences in our understanding of who God is, and how God enters our lives. We urge Friends to wrestle, as many of us have here, with the conviction and experience of many Friends throughout our history that this Inward Teacher is in fact Christ himself. We have been struck this week, however, with the experience of being forced to recognise this same God at work in others who call that Voice by different names, or who understand differently who that Voice is.

We have often wondered whether there is anything Quakers today can say as one. After much struggle we have discovered that we can proclaim this: there is a living God at the centre of all, who is available to each of us as a Present Teacher at the very heart of our lives. We seek as people of God to be worthy vessels to deliver the Lord's transforming word, to be prophets of joy who know from experience and can testify to the world, as George Fox did, `that the Lord God is at work in this thick night'. Our priority is to be receptive and responsive to the life-giving Word of God, whether it comes through the written word - the Scriptures, the

Incarnate Word - Jesus Christ, the Corporate Word - as discerned by the gathered meeting, or the Inward Word of God in our hearts which is available to each of us who seek the Truth.

This can be made easier if we face the truth within ourselves, embrace the pain, and lay down our differences before God for the Holy Spirit to forgive, thus transforming us into instruments of healing. This priority is not merely an abstract idea, but something we have experienced powerfully at work among us this week.

Our five invited speakers presented vivid pictures of economic, ecological and military crisis in this world today. We acknowledge that these crises are in fact only a reflection of the great spiritual crisis which underlies them all. Our peace testimony inspires us, yet we move beyond it to challenge our world with the call for justice. We are called to be peacemakers, not protestors.

It is our desire to work co-operatively on unifying these points. The challenges of this time are almost too great to be faced, but we must let our lives mirror what is written on our hearts - to be so full of God's love that we can do no other than live out our corporate testimonies to the world of honesty, simplicity, equality and peace, whatever the consequences.

We pray for both the personal and inner strength as well as the corporate strength of a shared calling/struggle that will empower us to face all the trials that we will necessarily encounter. We have no illusions about the fact that to truly live a Christian life in these cataclysmic times means to live a life of great risk.

We call on Friends to rediscover our own roots in the vision and lives of early Friends whose own transformed lives shook the unjust social and economic structures of their day. They treasured the records of God's encounters with humanity found in the Bible, and above all, the life and teachings of Jesus Christ. And we call upon Friends across the earth to heed the voice of God and let it send us out in truth and power to rise to the immense challenge of our world today.

Index of yearly meetings quoted